THE
Archive Photographs
SERIES

CODSALL
AND
CLAREGATE

St Nicholas' Church, Codsall, set on a hill overlooking the village with a horse chestnut tree just outside the gate, a tree where generations of Codsall children collected their conkers on their way to school. Sadly this magnificent tree has had to be removed recently and is replaced by a sapling.

An aerial view of Claregate garage, the focal point of the suburb for many years, but completely rebuilt since this photograph was taken in the 1960s.

THE
Archive Photographs
SERIES

CODSALL
AND
CLAREGATE

Compiled by
Alec Brew

CHALFORD

The Chalford Publishing Company
St Mary's Mill, Chalford,
Stroud, Gloucestershire, GL6 8NX

ISBN 0 7524 0674 8

Typesetting and origination by
The Chalford Publishing Company
Printed in Great Britain by
Redwood Books, Trowbridge

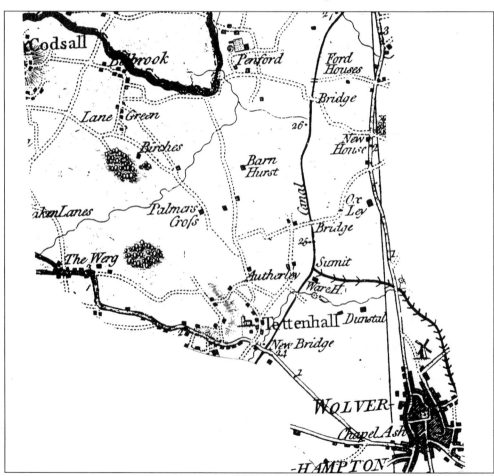

An eighteenth-century map of the area covered by this book which includes the districts between the Stafford road and Tettenhall, going out to the village of Codsall and its neighbours. Note the warehouse at the recently completed canal junction then known as Autherley, before the Shropshire Union Canal had even been built.

Contents

A 1906 drawing of part of the lost village of Aldersley, at the junction of the Birmingham Canal and the Staffordshire and Worcester. The four cottages to the left, and the toll-house to the right, were demolished in the 1960s, but the connecting wall and bridge still remain.

'

Wolverhampton Corporation's No. 15 bus, the 'Codsall via Claregate', about to start out from Victoria Square. It is a 1954 Guy Arab IV, built in Wolverhampton. The No. 15 bus played an important part in the dramatic changes in the area covered by this book, enabling people to live in the suburbs and villages and commute to work in the town.

Introduction

Two hundred years ago to the north of the small town of Wolverhampton were a handful of tiny villages, the largest of which was Oaken. In recent years it has been overtaken in population size by its near neighbour, Codsall. Anyone leaving Wolverhampton by the narrow meandering lanes which lay between the busier Stafford and Newport roads, would have been well into the countryside before even crossing the Smestow Brook in the valley between Wolverhampton and Tettenhall ridge, and would then have climbed over the hill by Palmer's Cross to the rural tranquillity beyond.

The first major change to the area came in 1772 with the opening of the Staffordshire and Worcester Canal, the first major East-West transport link across Britain. In the same year the Birmingham Canal Navigations also opened, linked to the Staffs and Worcester, at what was then known as Autherley Junction. Alongside Autherley Farm it later became Aldersley Junction when the start of the Shropshire Union Canal at Barnhurst adopted the title Autherley Junction.

For a time Aldersley Junction was arguably the most important inland transport junction in the world. For the first time coal from the Black Country mines could be transported in bulk to the West coast via Stourport and the Severn, and to the East coast and Merseyside via Great Haywood and the Trent and Mersey canal. Upwards of 100 boats a day passed up or down the twenty-one locks to Wolverhampton carrying the coal and then the iron and steel products of the emerging Black Country industries.

A village sprang up at Aldersley, with Canal Company offices, houses, and a warehouse, adding to the farming community which already existed, with Autherley Farm, Carr's Farm, and Blakeley Green House on one side of the canal, and Dunstall Hall and its associated buildings, including a water mill, on the other. The canals were overtaken by the railways, however, and Aldersley

Junction became an isolated backwater. The village itself has now disappeared, apart from a few cellar walls.

The Shrewsbury and Birmingham Railway which came through the area in 1849, brought the next major changes, as it became possible for wealthier people to work in Wolverhampton and to commute from large country houses they built near to Codsall station.

After the First World War new factories came into the area, most notably Courtaulds in Hordern Road and Boulton Paul Aircraft, lured to a green-field site next to the new Wolverhampton Municipal Airport at Pendeford. Boulton Paul had an instant effect because the company brought 600 workers and their families with them from Norwich. Houses were built for them in Bilbrook, Claregate and Fordhouses, an instant population increase of 2,000 East Anglians. At the same time the boundaries of Wolverhampton were spreading ever outward down Hordern Road, up through Claregate and over the hill.

The biggest single change in the area was wrought by the No. 15 bus, Wolverhampton Corporation's 'Codsall via Claregate' route. For the first time ordinary people could live in the suburbs and villages and commute to work in the town, though my own grandfather 'commuted on foot' from Codsall to Oxley Sidings for a while after the Great War - until he could afford a bicycle. More housing estates sprang up to house these new commuters, a process which was accelerated after the Second World War with the advent of wider car ownership.

I grew up in the 1950s in Oaken, a village of farms and large country houses with a few scattered cottages. The farms have become 'barn conversions', the cows have disappeared from the fields to be replaced by ponies for the people who live in the barn conversions and the large houses are slowly becoming Nursing Homes. The gaps between cottages have been filled with new houses and the Post Office shop has closed.

This is a process echoed throughout the area, and only one field physically separates Codsall, Bilbrook and Birches Bridge, now coalesced into one large village, from being another suburb of Wolverhampton, like Claregate and its neighbouring districts.

Separated by the county boundary, Codsall and Claregate, and their neighbouring areas, are still linked by railway and bus but most of all they are linked by the shared experiences of the people who live there, experiences this book attempts to recall.

One

Codsall

Suffering the fate of most rural villages located just too near a large town, Codsall has become a residential district for its larger neighbour, Wolverhampton. Though still surrounded by fields and farms, the village began to lose its rural character between the wars, a process which accelerated rapidly in the fifties and sixties, as new housing estates were built, filling up all the gaps until Codsall/Bilbrook/Birches Bridge had become a village conurbation.

Nevertheless it is an ancient parish spreading south of St Nicholas' church, down the hill to Moat Brook, which probably took its name from the medieval moated farms of Moor Hall and Wood Hall. The railway brought wealthy families from Wolverhampton and the Black Country, to build large country houses from which they could commute and later brought day-trippers from the Black Country, as the village became a popular day out.

Codsall Square before the First World War and looking fairly busy. Everyone has been asked by the photographer to stand still. The horse and cart is coming up Wood Road, past the Crown. There is a wagon outside York's Stores, on the left.

Codsall football team for the season 1897/98. At a guess the large gentleman on the left was the manager, but none of the names are known.

A Bible study class on the vicarage lawn c. 1912. The only person that can be named is standing ninth from the left and is William George Fox, who was born in 1895, and whose father was a porter on the railway. He lived in the end house of Railway Terrace.

A view looking up Church Road before the Great War. The by-pass now runs through the foreground, but Bakers House, on the left is still in use as Russell House.

Further up Church Road at the same time. The entrance and wall to Manor Court on the left still remain, but all the buildings on the other side of the road have gone. Note that the road was cobbled at the time. It is believed the cobbles still remain under the tarmac.

Members of the Codsall Working Men's Club on Coronation Day 1911, probably in Wood Road. The only name known is William J.L. Fox, (seated, second left) well known for being a jovial sort of man and for playing the squeeze box.

Betty Baron (Hardcastle) as Queen of the May, in the days when celebrating May Day was a big event in Codsall.

Oaken Lanes used to be prone to flooding. This photograph was taken by Dr Burd, the village doctor, in around 1910.

A view of Landsdown Avenue from the top before any houses had been built. At the time there was a large quarry to the left, across which a footbridge ran.

Codsall Station before the First World War, with the station staff lined up. The railway was built around 1849 and brought the first commuters to Codsall and beginning the process of change.

Station Road, with Railway Terrace on the left seen sometime before the First World War.

The station staff in the 1930s. Seen, left to right, are: Mr Evans (stationmaster), unknown porter, Harry Richards (signalman) and, sitting down, Terry Evans, the stationmaster's son.

Mill Lane with the church and vicarage alongside. Actually taken in 1952, this scene has remained little changed, and generations of schoolchildren, myself included, have been galvanised into action by the sound of the school bell, while trooping up this back way.

The class of eight year olds at St Nicholas' School in 1913. Mr Ullyett, the headmaster, is on the left, he served as head from 1907 to 1933.

A view of the school from Mill Lane, in 1952, with the bicycle sheds down the middle of the playground, separating boys from girls. The outside toilets are on the right.

The infants I class in September 1919, with the teacher, Mrs Barley. There are exactly seventeen boys and seventeen girls.

Another school group taken in September 1923, posing in the playground by the wall with Mill House.

A village celebration, probably before the First World War. The children are lined up in the school playground, with the Mill House visible behind, and are probably celebrating Empire Day as they seemed to be dressed up as all the nationalities under the sun.

The staff at Baker's Nurseries taken around 1919. Some of them are dressed in bits of military uniforms, including one in a German army cap! William George Fox in the middle row, fourth from the right, with Hubert Veale over his right shoulder.

George Russell (left) in 1931, with his famous lupins in Baker's Nurseries. With him are Harry Law, who looked after the roses, and his son, also called Harry.

Miss Lilian Beatrice Picken of New Home Farm, Codsall, with Prince Alexander Bariatinsky and his brother. For twelve years Miss Picken worked in Russia as companion to Princess Bariatinsky, the youngest daughter of Tsar Alexander II. She was caught up in the Revolution and following a harrowing escape, returned to Codsall in 1919 where the Princes later visited her.

Mr Caulkin of the Croft Diary, Sandy Lane, Codsall, photographed in Hadden Hill.

Lansdown Avenue in the 1930s, now a quiet residential avenue, looking towards Chapel Lane.

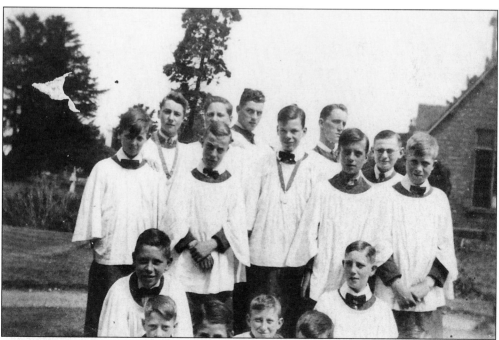

Codsall Church choir in the churchyard, with the school behind them, in the 1930s. Back row, left to right: Eric Evans, -?-, Richard Slaney, Harry Evans, Ron Pritchard. Second row: Gordon Wilson, Ernie Butters, Frank Wilson, Les Rogers, Harold Meredith. Third row: Andrew Moody, -?-. Front row: Harry Law, -?-, Stan Illidge, -?-.

The marriage of John Henry Law of Moorlands Farm, Pattingham, to Evelyn Rowley at the Mind, Histons Hill on 18 June 1921.

The Crown at the Wergs, with some of the locals relaxing with their pints by the lawn.

Wergs Hall taken in 1934 when it was in possession of the Swanson family. It had been built around 1860 by the Fryer family. In 1963 it was bought by Sir Aldred MacAlpine & Son Ltd, for use as their offices, with large new extensions on the side. It has now been sold to Tarmac Ltd.

The Wergs Platoon of the Home Guard being inspected in December 1940. The Wergs Platoon was part of 'C' Company. Left to right: Major H.R. Culliwick, -?- (captain), Captain Parker (OC 24 Battalion), Lord Dartmouth, CSM Slater, Lieut. F.P. Webster (Platoon CO).

The Codsall Platoon of the Home Guard with Colonel Parkes in the centre, 1942. The Codsall Home Guard formed 'A' Company.

The whole of the Codsall Home Guard, date and location unknown, although it might have been around the time of the stand down in 1944.

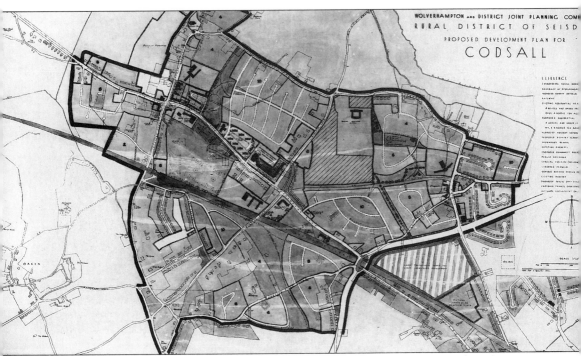

The proposed development plan for Codsall dated 1947. The actuality turned out rather different. The wide by-pass over Birches Bridge was never built, the area of the Wheel estate shows just sports pitches, and the 'Light Industrial Development' in the shaded area south of Duck Lane never happened. However, the outer boundary has been largely largely followed.

An aerial view of Codsall from above Oaken in the 1950s showing just what a small, rural village it was. The houses are in Broadway/Chapel Lane, and the Square in to the left.

Codsall Secondary Modern School, as it was in 1952. It was built as Codsall Senior Mixed School in 1940 and is now Codsall High School.

School staff in 1946. Back row, left to right: Mr W. Chetwood, Mr L.G. Franks, Mr Jones, Mr A. Smeaton, Miss J. Kingshott, Mr E. McDonnell, Mrs Roberts. Seated: Miss Leach, Mrs Morris, Mr G.E. Gibbs (headmaster), Mrs E. Dewey, Miss M. Orton.

An aerial view of Codsall taken in 1953, showing the Square on the left and Church Road. Baker's Nurseries are prominent, as is the farm in the foreground.

An aerial view of the church taken at the same time, with the school on the left.

The Secondary Modern School staff *c*. 1950. Standing, left to right: -?-, -?-, -?-, -?-, Mr Bould, Miss Kingshott, Mr Mansell, -?-, Miss Orton, Mr Robinson, -?-, -?-, Mr Millington. Seated: -?-, Miss Morton, Mrs Wright, Mrs Dewey, Mr Gibbs, Mr Franks, Mr Smeaton, Mrs Porteous, Miss Till.

Mr Wilkinson teaching geography at the Secondary Modern School in the mid 1950s.

A small road roller being used for repairs to Histons Hill in 1952.

Codsall Cubs and Scouts in 1953. The Codsall Troop had originated in the early twenties, and their HQ was initially at the Rifle Range, Wood Road. They then occupied a loft over the stables of the Mount and settled, finally, where they are depicted here in their own scout hut in Wood Road.

The Codsall Forget-Me-Not Club on fire in 1968. The firemen failed to save it.

A geography field studies trip from the Secondary Modern School seen here camping in Yorkshire in 1954. Mr Wilkinson is at the left rear, with Mr Mansell (the PE teacher) to the right at the back.

The senior class of Codsall Primary School in the churchyard with Mr Wilkins, their teacher, in 1964.

A year group at the Secondary Modern School, *c.* 1956.

Denis Housden's shop in Codsall Square in the 1960s. It had a number of previous owners including A.L. Harvey and J. Reynolds and was the first shop in Codsall laid out in supermarket style.

The area on the Wolverhampton Road which was re-developed with eight new shops in the 1960s. The two small shops are Housden's fruit and florists and E.B. Jenkins drapers. The old cottage was formerly a chapel.

The oldest cottage in Codsall, now the Indian restaurant. It is usually, erroneously, called the Manor House. It was narrowly saved from demolition when the by-pass was built.

The bottom of Church Road in the 1960s just before the by-pass was built.

The top of Church Road in 1961. All the buildings on the right have been demolished, including the sweet shop, a regular stopping point for all children on their way to school, including myself!

The Co-op butchers shop at the top of Church Road with Eddie Griffiths standing outside his cottage. Both buildings have long since been demolished.

Codsall Square looking down Station Road, with Stanton's Store (formerly York's) in the centre. Lloyd's Bank is behind. The cottages on the left were demolished to make way for new shops.

The ford in Moat Brook Lane, which has since been replace by a culvert. It was very useful for car washing.

The Codsall Secondary Modern School prefects for the year 1969/70.

The check-out staff of the Concord supermarket in 1969. Concord was sited where the Post Office is now.

A former
Wolverhampton
Corporation Guy
Arab Mk.IV 'full-
fronted' bus, in
WMPTE colours
negotiating the
tight corner from
Station Road on a
rail replacement
service. Stanton's
Store has now been
taken over by
Lloyd's Bank,
which later moved
to join the new
shops.

An Inter-City train running through Codsall Station towards Shrewsbury in the 1970s. Now a
rare sight as Inter-City starts in Wolverhampton.

Half-time during a Conservative Club mixed football match, *c*. 1980.

The Codsall Showband in 1972, who were mostly pupils from what had become Codsall Comprehensive School. Their line up included: Nigel Yates (sax), Peter Scott (flute), Nigel Addison, Claire Maltby, Andrew Mansell, John Law, Paul Lind (clarinets), Neil Bradley, Alison Sharp (trumpets), Peter Grosvenor (cello), David Hickman (drums), David Yates (sound effects), Laurence Smallwood (piano).

Two
Codsall Wood

A much smaller village than Codsall, Codsall Wood grew on an area of waste land on the rising ground to the north west, hard by Chillington Hall. Reliant on its neighbour for much of its sustenance, including the school, Codsall Wood has nevertheless retained a strong individual identity, without being too parochial.

It has long been a destination for visitors from the Black Country, its four pubs benefitting from the rule which allowed bona fide travellers, i.e. those who had gone more than three miles, to get a drink on a Sunday. Its pubs are down to two, but the visitors still come, and the annual Flower Show at Pendrell Hall is just one example of village togetherness.

The Crown in Codsall Wood some time before the First World War. This was one of five pubs in the village at the time, three of which have gone, and this building has since been replaced by a new one.

Cottages in Codsall Wood, c. 1908. The ones on the right still stand, as does the building behind the lady, which says, 'Tea provided'. The cottage behind that has gone.

Mr and Mrs Blake outside Bath Farm, on the Chillington Estate at Codsall Wood.

The Lodge at the Codsall Wood entrance to Chillington Hall, in 1907.

Chillington Hall in 1907, the seat of the Giffard Family, and sited nearer to Codsall Wood, though located in Brewood Parish.

Boscobel House the famous hiding place of King Charles when on the run from the Parliamentary forces after the Battle of Worcester, lies hard by Codsall Wood. This view of the farmyard, before the Great War, is unusual, as most photographs show the house.

The peculiar summer house of Boscobel House, built on a mound in the garden, and looking much the same today, in this photograph taken around eighty years earlier.

This old oak tree lay outside the gates to Pendrell Hall in Codsall Wood and was much photographed. It should not be confused with the 'King's Oak' at Boscobel.

The May Fair in the grounds of Pendrell Hall in 1927. Mr Gaskell is standing alongside the May Queen's throne. The Gaskell family owned Pendrell Hall for many years.

Levi Brown with a cart load of mangels at Heath Hayes Farm, Codsall Wood, sometime between the wars.

The farmyard at Wheatstone Lodge between the wars. The man in the centre is William Brown, stockman for Wood Hall Farm.

An aerial view of Codsall Wood taken in 1953. The Crown is the building by the roadside on the right.

Coronation celebrations at Codsall Wood in June 1953. Some of the spectators, standing left to right are: Minnie Hodson (of Whitehouse Farm), Jack Davies, Mrs Wall, Bill Matthews, Mrs Matthews, Mrs Laurie Davies, Winnie Houghton and Paul Davies is the child in fancy dress.

Another group at the Codsall Wood Coronation celebrations in 1953.

The Codsall Wood Flower Show was a regular village event and is seen here in 1960.

Three

Oaken

Built on a rival hill on the other side of Moat Brook, Oaken has at times been a bigger settlement than its neighbour, Codsall. Only in the nineteenth century did Codsall expand greatly beyond the size of its southern neighbour, and the reasons why are not easy to fathom; even when the railway came it passed between the two.

The lack of a church in Oaken is strange, though there may one have been one on the adjacent Wrottesley Park Estate, and the only inn is the Foaming Jug, a long way from the centre on the Newport road, but there may have been others long ago. Though it retains its tranquillity Oaken has paid the price, the shop in Shop Lane closed long ago, and now even the post office is gone.

A drawing of Oaken Lanes, showing one of Oaken Manor Farm's barns on the left. The wall of the Fold is on the right and what is now March Cottage straight ahead.

The centre of Oaken before the First World War. The Post Office is on the right, with the smithy beyond. The wall of the terrace is on the left.

The corner of Oaken Lanes and Middle Lane before the roads were paved, showing Oaken Manor Farmhouse, which has now been replaced by a new building. Judging by the chimneys, the original building may well have been Tudor. The farm behind has recently been converted into cottages.

Haymaking in one of the fields around Oaken. Perhaps one of the horses has a fly in its ear, judging by the head shaking!

Strawmoor Farm on the corner of Oaken Lanes and Jug Lane before 1917. The waggoner is Mr Head seen here with his son and son-in-law. He worked for Mr Jones the farmer. The farm still looks much as it did but the house had been doubled in size.

OLD COTTAGE OAKEN

An old cottage in Oaken, opposite Oaken Manor, now known as the Thatch. Though now much enlarged, it is invisible from the road because of its hedge.

Oaken Avenue, more usually called Oaken Drive, which leads to Springfield House and then, Oaken. The lodge is still there and was known as Witches Cottage when I was a boy. I walked bravely passed it every day on my way to Codsall School!

George and Elizabeth Brew outside the Fold in Oaken, c. 1894. The baby is my grandfather, James Daniel Brew, and his elder brother, on his father's knee, was named George. He died when he was seven years old. George snr. was a veteran of the Zulu Wars and worked in a quarry in Histons Hill.

Dan Brew when he was about sixteen years old and just out of Codsall School. He worked at the Manor, the Terrace and Greenhills Farm before joining his father in the quarry and later going on the railway.

Jane Macham, a maid at Oaken Manor just before the First World War. After the war she married Dan Brew and went to live with her father-in-law, then living in Suckling Green Lane, where my father was subsequently born.

A Fordson Tractor fitted with a prototype Perkins diesel engine on trial at Wrottesley Park, Oaken, in the summer of 1937, prior to the Royal Show being held there. Reginald Tildesley, the Fordson dealer is fifth from the left. The others are local farmers and salesmen.

Oaken Manor Farm's milk delivery van in the 1930s. The farm was owned by W.M. Illiff, who lived in Oaken Manor, but the farm was run by a bailiff who lived in the farmhouse.

Oaken Post Office, date unknown. This picture is something of a mystery. Either the post office had a front garden which was later removed, or this is a different, but almost identical, building.

A cottage in Shop Lane, Oaken, now removed and replace by bungalows. In the gateway are June Vaughan, Lily Vaughan, Thomas Vaughan and little Alice Vaughan, who was born in 1908.

The stables at Oaken Riding School which were attached to The Cedars at Cater's Corner at the bottom of The Hollybush. Mr W. Carter and his sister, Phyllis, are in the foreground.

The officers of the 24th Battalion, Home Guard, at a party at the Manor House, Oaken, in May 1942. Colonel Parkes, who lived in the Manor House was the CO of the Battalion.

Another Home Guard party at the Manor House, on Whit Saturday 1944, this time for the officers and their wives.

Haymaking in Oaken in 1949, with rather more modern equipment than the earlier photograph, including an elevator to load the wagon.

An aerial view of Oaken taken in 1953, with Middle Lane on the right and Oaken Manor in the foreground. Shop Lane is on the top right.

The Oaken Coronation celebrations in June 1953, outside the Post Office. The author is on the extreme left.

George Withnall and Peter Brew passing Charlesfield, Oaken in about 1958. George was tractor-driver for Oaken Manor Farm and usually drove this red David Brown.

Mrs Leah Brew driving an Allis-Chalmers tractor in the late fifties. She often helped out on the Illiff's farm during the busy seasons. As a nine year old I also drove the tractor during the harvest time and was told to swear blind I was thirteen, if anyone asked.

Four
Birches and Bilbrook

Before the coming of the Railway the area covered by these villages was almost entirely rural with a few large estates, notably The Birches, and Bilbrook Manor, and one inn, the Woodman, on Lane Green. The railway created a new name, Birches Bridge, and by the bridge grew a new centre for the area, with a garage and most of the shops, and, in 1934, a new station, Birches and Bilbrook Halt.

The expansion of Bilbrook into a large village was already underway after Boulton Paul Aircraft began its move from Norwich in 1936 to a new factory at Pendeford, a quarter of a mile away. Bilbrook became almost a Company village as the Norfolk men, and new employees, moved there. Later still the area coalesced with Codsall as new housing developments filled all the gaps, and it became a residential area for Wolverhampton and the Black Country.

A group outside Bilbrook Manor House around 1865. Left to right: Sam Fellows, his sister, Edgar Fellows, Ted Jones.

An aerial view of Bilbrook Manor taken in 1938 from an aircraft flying from Pendeford. Bilbrook Road runs alongside it and Bilbrook Manor Park estate now occupies the site.

Bilbrook Manor, which was owned during this century by the Twentyman family and demolished in 1945.

The entrance to Bilbrook Manor on Bilbrook Road with Bickerton's Cottage and the start of Joey's Lane to the right.

The Albrighton Hunt gathered on Lane Green outside the Woodman Inn. The right hand end of the building, at this time, was apparently still a barn.

Ernest Gaskell on the knee of his grandfather, J. Holbrook, at the Birches, in 1908. The Birches was another of the Gaskells' residences.

The rear of the Birches Farm, alongside the Wolverhampton Road, some time before 1910. The adults in the picture were Worskett, the coachman, and his wife.

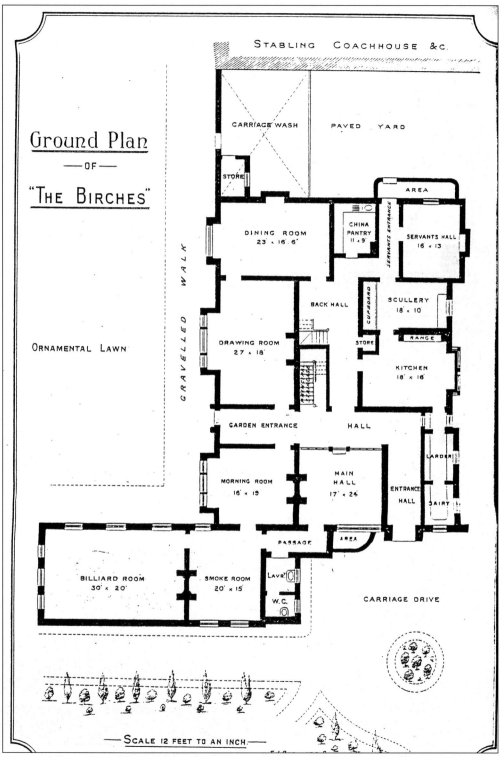

A ground floor plan of the Birches when it was sold as part of the Wergs Hall Estate in 1907.

William Smith, the gardener from the Birches, and his wife, Ellen, outside their cottage at Dam Mill, which sits in the fork between the Wolverhampton road and Lane Green Road.

The Woodman in the 1930s. The barn on the right has been incorporated into the pub with long windows in the area of the double doors.

LOT 5.

(Coloured Blue on Plan.)

The Birches Farm.

A modern substantial, and commodious Farm House of two stories, in the Gothic style, with ample Farm Buildings, Cottages, &c.

THE BIRCHES FARM HOUSE.

Residence.   The house contains—dining, drawing, and morning rooms, large kitchen, scullery, larder or dairy, 8 bed and dressing rooms, bath room with bath, and 3 cellars, with coal place, out-offices, and enclosed yard at the rear.

There is a lawn and garden, and timber trees and shrubs surround the house.

Farm Buildings.   The Farm Buildings, which are arranged round a large fold yard, consist of feeding houses for 26 cattle, large double barn, stabling for 7 horses with loft, brick and tile cart sheds, cart shed with room over, lean-to iron shed, Hackney stable, harness room, piggeries, &c. There is also a nearly new **Dutch Barn** of steel and corrugated iron.

Land   The Farm is divided into convenient fields of rich pasture, meadow, and arable; the whole being in an excellent state of cultivation, and in the occupation of Mr. E. J. Jones as yearly tenant,

Cottages.   also two pairs of recently erected semi-detached **Cottages** fronting the Codsall Road, near to the railway bridge, with gardens, &c., and pump and well for water supply. Two of these houses contain 4, and the others 5 rooms each, and there are the requisite out-offices adjoining.

Keeper's Cottage.   There is also another 2-story Brick and Tile Cottage called "Bedford Cottage," or "The Keeper's Lodge," fronting the road from Wergs to the Birches, containing 2 living rooms, pantry, 3 bedrooms, and washhouse, with several brick and tile sheds; a boiling house with iron roof, dog kennels, aviary and other buildings outside, with a large and productive garden attached. No. 63 on Plan.

Note as to Road.   Lot 5 will be sold subject to the right of the purchaser of Lot 4 to a joint use of the road in common between the points of **A** and **B** on plan, the respective purchasers of Lots 4 and 5 covenanting jointly to maintain and repair such road.

Tenure.   This Lot is copyhold of the Manor of the Deanery of Wolverhampton, except as stated in Note to Lot 4.

	A	R	P	£	s.	d.
The Tenancies of this lot are divided as follows: Mr. E. J. Jones ...189	3	35		319	10	0
apportioned Rental						
Sir Alfred Hickman, Bart. ...	0	2	2	10	0	0

The apportioned Shooting Rent on Lot 5 is £13 per annum.

The commuted tithe is £58 0s. 3d. per annum.

The land tax, £4 19s. 9d. per annum.

FOR REFERENCE TO PLAN OF LOT 5 (see over).

A page of the catalogue of the Wergs Hall Estate sale in 1907 showing Birches Farm and its associated buildings.

An aerial view of the camouflaged Boulton Paul Aircraft factory, during the War, with four Defiants on the apron. Built in 1936 it was soon enlarged. Many of its labour force lived in Bilbrook, which can be seen in the background. Pendeford Mill Pool, on the right, also seems to have been camouflaged in some way.

The Lane Green shops and Post Office just before the War. There were no buildings on the other side of the road at this time.

The Home Guard's Nuttall flame-thrower, which was designed by Captain Wood and built by CSM Nuttall. It had a 50 gallon tank on an Austin 7 chassis and gave a 75 ft flame for 3 minutes. Its usual base was under the bridge at Dam Mill (in case the Germans came down the road from Bilbrook, I suppose).

Boulton Paul Aircraft drawing office staff outside the Woodman, which was the local pub, in the late 1940s.

Lane Green Post Office not long after it opened in the 1930s. The red phone box and cigarette machine have now gone.

The last Inter-City train through Birches and Bilbrook Halt in 1993. The photograph is of a 'down' train taken from the 'up' platform.

Five

Claregate and Aldersley

As can be seen from the picture below, at the turn of the century Claregate hardly existed at all as a community. It was a farming region except for the small village of Aldersley, the group of canal-buildings around Aldersley Junction, with the nearby Autherley Farm, Carr's Farm, and Blakeley Green House, making a scattered little settlement.

The expansion of Wolverhampton began to take over the area between the wars, making Aldersley, Claregate and Palmer's Cross one large suburb, centred on the junction on the Codsall Road where Claregate Island was built, alongside Claregate garage and Post Office. Conversely the village of Aldersley disappeared, with only Blakeley Green House surviving.

The view from the centre of Claregate before the First World War, and, at that time, a very rural scene. Taken from what is now Claregate Island it shows the old Fieldhouse pub in the distance. Two workers in the 'John E. Knight' nursery are watching over the hedge. Knight's Avenue now runs through this area.

A horse-drawn bus outside the old Fieldhouse at Claregate, which seems to have been run by Horace Barkin, late of Horseley Fields.

A slightly later group picture, occasion unknown, taken outside the Fieldhouse, which was replaced between the Wars with a much larger building.

Part of 'the lost village of Aldersley' at the start of the Birmingham Canal Navigations on the junction with the Staffs and Worcs canal which was opened in 1772. The building is the BCN toll-house, lock keeper's cottages and offices. For a time this was one of the busiest and most important inland transport junctions in the world with upwards of 100 boats a day passing through.

The terrace of four cottages at Aldersley Junction, two of which were lived in, in later years, by the canal workers, Mr Hughes and Mr Jackson. The others were leased. The arch on the right hand side of the bridge lead down to the stables in the cellars of the cottages, which can still be seen today. All the buildings at Aldersley were demolished around 1960.

The 400 year old Autherley Farm, on the other bank of the canal from the Aldersley Junction buildings, sometime between the wars. This too has been demolished to make a new entrance for Aldersley Stadium. Two of the barns remain.

The entrance to Autherley Farm, or Picken's Farm as it was known. Beyond the gate is the lane and then the railway to Wombourne. The lane ran under the railway, passed the farm and then went over a bridge back to Aldersley Road, which can be seen in the background.

Fred and Gwyneth Picken and their son Andy, outside the farmhouse between the wars.

Fred Picken was very keen on horse riding and is seen here on his farm which was on a rise above the canal. All of this land is now forms part of the Aldersley Stadium sports complex.

Claregate Post Office, next off the island, at the top of Blackburn Avenue. It was then called 'Speed's shop'.

The shops in Green Lane just after construction in 1938. The start of Blakeley Avenue can be seen, and the trees are growing in what is now the middle of Green Lane. Mr Bates the butcher has already occupied the first shop and Mrs Price the newsagent is next door, but Cuthbert's the builders were using what is now the hairdressers as a site office.

£5 SECURES.   **£30 TOTAL DEPOSIT.**

"TYPE "C"

FREEHOLD from **£525** "all-in."

* Dining Room with French Casement opening into Garden.
* Sitting Room with large Bay.
* Modern Kitchen with Cabinet and Cooking Range.
* Spacious Hall with covered Entrance Porch.
* Front Bedroom with large Bay, Coal Fireplace.
* Large Second Bedroom, Electric Fire installed.
* Third Bedroom sufficiently large for a 4ft. bedstead.
* Bathroom with Panelled Bath, Wash-basin, W.C. and
  Linen Cupboard.
* Wireless and Power Points installed.
* Outside Brick-built Coal House.
* Concrete Paths and Garage Space.

A page from the Blakeley Green Estate catalogue showing No. 24 Blakeley Avenue, which was for sale for £525 'all in'. Other houses were available for £499, 'all in'.

Fred Picken as depicted in the Co-op seed catalogue with his prize 30-40 lb mangelwurzels. Mangels were a common cattle feed crop on farms in those days.

Fred Picken and a pile of mangels by the railway bridge on Oxley Moor Road, at one end of 'Three Corner Field' surrounded on all three sides by the railway. It is now used by Wolverhampton & Bilston Athletic Club for hammer throwing and shot-put practice. His two labourers probably had aching backs after topping and tailing 30-40 lb mangels all day!

A Deans Goods No. 2516 local hauling a Stephenson Locomotive Society special along the south side of Fred Picken's 'Three Corner Field', from Oxley North Junction on the line to Tettenhall and Wombourne on 31 May 1955. This line is now the Valley Park footpath.

Oxley North Junction in July 1962, looking north to what is now the Dovecotes Estate, as the ex-GWR *King George V*, No. 6000, hauls the Birkenhead to Paddington Express.

Claregate garage, probably just after the War, when it was apparently a BP/National Benzole outlet. During the War it was used for sub-contract war work.

One of the colony of 600 Norfolk families who moved to the area with Boulton Paul Aircraft in 1936. Billy Holmes and his wife are shown outside No. 47 Blackburn Avenue. Peering round the door are their sons, Jack and Brian, with friend, Cyril Plimmer. All three became Boulton Paul apprentices.

A VE Day street party in Blackburn Avenue, Claregate, outside No. 117. They could not sit here long these days before being run down.

Three gardeners on the allotments which used to occupy the area behind Burland Avenue now covered by the car park of the Claregate pub. Left to right: Percival (Sax) Dewey of No. 64 Burland Avenue, Harold Young of No. 15 Codsall Road, Fred Edwards of No. 107 Burland Avenue. The allotment holders used the Smoke Room of what was then the Fieldhouse, almost as a private club room.

Claregate Old Boys football team, ex-Youth Club in Hordern Road, *c.* 1950. For a while they had a pitch on Picken's Farm, and had to fill in a ditch across it before they could use it. Back row, left to right: Arthur Broome, Bill Sharples, Denis Richards, Gerald Morris, Brian Holmes, Des Middleton, Derek Leighton, Bill Richards, John Gaiger. Front row: Roy Barnett, Doug Shelton, Lionel Rutter, Jeff Wassall, Bill Gillespie.

Claregate garage before re-development, showing the entrance to the workshop which used to occupy the rear of the building.

Two ex-London Transport buses, owned by Central Coachways, parked in Lynton Avenue in June 1964, after bringing a party to Aldersley Stadium

Roy Downing, who lived in No. 121 Blackburn Avenue, outside the Fieldhouse in 1955. Now, of course, the pub has been renamed, with astonishing imagination, 'The Claregate'!

Burland Avenue, Claregate, winning the FA Cup in 1949! Billy Wright holds the cup and to his left, Jesse Pye and Terry Springthorpe, all lodged at No. 98 Burland Avenue. This is, of course, Wolverhampton Wanderer's victorious team having just beaten Leicester 3-1.

Billy Wright with some of his 105 England caps in Mrs Colley's front room, No. 98 Burland Avenue. It's hard to conceive of today's England captain lodging in a three bedroom semi-detached.

Billy Wright (centre) at the back of No. 98 Burland Avenue with Mr and Mrs Colley, on his left, their son Arthur and Peggy Taylor who lived in Blackburn Avenue, and later married a Dutchman.

A year group at Palmer's Cross County Primary School, c. 1960. Palmer's Cross was built between 1952 and 1955, a very attractive and well-built school by more recent standards and named after a cross at which Palmer's (holy men who went on the Crusades) are supposed to have prayed.

Another year group in 1962 at the front of the building which is on Windermere Road in an area often called 'The Lake District', because of the names of the roads.

Palmer's Cross football team for the year 1962.

The No. 34 bus waiting to start its return journey outside the Pilot public house in Green Lane, Claregate in 1959. This is a Guy Arab IV and many of the people living in the area will have worked at Guy Motors and helped build it.

Billy Wright on *This is your Life* with Eamon Andrews. The lady's name was Helen, and she was the bus conductress on the No. 15 Codsall via Claregate bus. She was the one who told Billy he had been made Captain of England, when he climbed on her bus to go home from a 0-0 draw in Denmark.

The No. 15 outside The Claregate, which was Billy's stop. This is much later, in 1959, as it is Wolverhampton's first front entrance double-decker, a Guy Arab IV with a 68-seat body.

A No. 14 Claregate bus picking up passengers on Aldersley Avenue in 1960. Note the 'Aldersley Stadium' board above the grill, which was carried when important sporting events were taking place there.

The premises of Hallmacromes Ltd in Macrome Road, Claregate, shortly after it had closed. The main building is still in use, now with Rothley Tube, but the canteen and cricket pitch have gone and the space is occupied by Fern Plastics.

Chris Tarrant arriving at Palmer's Cross School in a Brantly B.2 helicopter after landing on the sports field.

Chris judging the Fancy Dress Competition.

The newest school in Claregate, Claregate Primary School in Chester Avenue, shown here around 1970. It was built on land which had previously been occupied by Carr's Farm, part of which is incorporated in the adjacent Aldersley House.

The first dinner ladies at Claregate School, in 1967. Left to right: Betty Price, Irene Walmsley, Kath Limb. The demountable (wooden) classrooms have yet to be built outside the children's entrance. Aldersley House, a residential home, is visible behind.

The Claregate School netball team in more recent years. Back row, left to right: Satvinder Goraya, Lorna Brown, Danielle Poxon, Emma Webb, Samantha Haywood, Yasmin ?, Hannah Landman, Helen Wincott.

Claregate garage celebrating its reopening after a total rebuild. The workshops were removed during the alterations.

Six

Fordhouses
and Pendeford

In 1934 the Norwich company of Boulton & Paul Ltd sold off its aircraft department, which became an independent company, Boulton Paul Aircraft Ltd, and began looking for a site for a new factory, next to an airfield. At about that time Wolverhampton took advice from Alan Cobham and decided to site its new Municipal Airport on Barnhurst Farm at Pendeford. Boulton Paul were offered a green field site, and began building its new factory in 1935.

Access to the airport and the new factory was provided by widening Wobaston Lane from Fordhouses, a village on the Stafford road, much of which was knocked down in the process. Fordhouses expanded to become a large suburb, which proved the undoing of the Airport when a Dowty Boulton Paul aircraft crashed on some of the new council houses in 1969. The Airport closed shortly after, and became the large new housing development of Pendeford, with a small business park where the airport buildings used to be.

The Stafford road, Fordhouses between the wars. The Vine public house is on the right and the cottage behind, and all the buildings on the left, were demolished before the War to widen the road.

The shops at Fordhouses before the War and the Stafford road looking towards Wolverhampton. Note the trolley bus wires overhead.

Another view of the cottages at Fordhouses, looking towards Stafford. The view from this spot would now take in the old Dana-Spicer factory and Lucas Aerospace beyond.

Another view of Fordhouses' shops, looking along Wobaston Lane in the days before there was a traffic island.

The Gate Inn on the Stafford road, which was knocked down when the road was widened in 1937. It was located near where the BP filling station is now sited.

An aerial view of Fordhouses taken in 1941, showing the Wobaston Road across the centre, leading to the Stafford road at the Vine junction on the left. Marston's factory can be seen alongside the Wobaston Road, but Hobson's and Turner's have yet to be built.

The start of Wobaston Lane between the wars, which petered out into a track at the top of Pendeford Hill. It was later widened to provide access to the new Municipal Airport at Pendeford and then Boulton Paul Aircraft. The houses on the left still stand but now face the factory which started as Turner's and then later became Dana-Spicer.

A map of the new Wolverhampton Municipal Airport at Pendeford from the official opening day programme in 1938. The new Boulton Paul factory was to the west around the other side of Pendeford Hill.

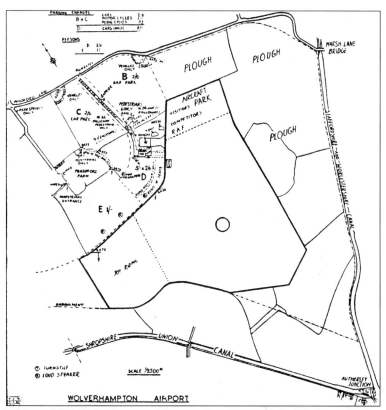

The Earl and Countess of Harrowby visiting Boulton Paul Aircraft on 29 October 1937. Back row, left to right: J.L. Wood (Company Secretary), Lord Gorell (Chairman), Mr H. Strickland (Managing Director), Mr H.E. Carter. Front row: Mrs J.L. Wood, Lady Gorell, Mrs J.D. North, the Earl and Countess of Harrowby, Viscountess Sandon, Mrs H.E. Carter, Mrs H. Strickland.

A Boulton Paul supervisor's outing, before the War. Most were Norfolk men, having moved with the Company from Norwich in 1936. A Don Everall coach is behind, but the location of the event is not known.

Blackburn Roc turret fighters in production before the War. All 136 Rocs were built by Boulton Paul, following on 106 Hawker Demons, the first aircraft built at Pendeford. It's said that those on Roc wing production earned exceptionally high bonuses which was a cause of much resentment for the rest of the firm.

The prototype of Boulton Paul's own Defiant fighter, outside the flight sheds behind the factory. Two squadrons of Defiants fought in the Battle of Britain, and it was the most successful night fighter during the months of the Blitz.

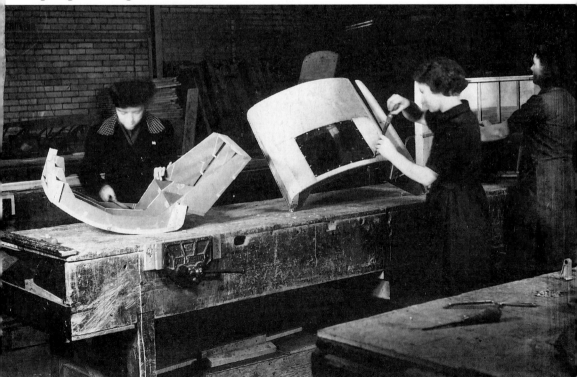

During the war the workforce expanded rapidly to nearly 5,000, many of whom were women. These workers are making the wooden turret fairings for the Defiant.

The Flight Shed interdepartmental cricket team just after the war. They are, back row, left to right: R. Elliott (umpire), L. Jelfs, N. Horne, Joe Plant (Rolls Royce rep), ? Nichols, F. Davies, S. Bunkell, -?- (umpire). Front row, T. Simpson, B. Brown, B. Elly, S. Davidge, -?-, S. Barber.

The flight shed team in 1942, including Chief Test Pilot Cecil Feather (in the flying helmet) at the time of the flight of the first of 692 Fairey Barracudas built by Boulton Paul.

An aerial view of Pendeford Airport during the war. It has been camouflaged with painted 'hedges' and 'trees'. New hangars for the RAF are being built at the bottom of the picture. Oxley Moor Road is top left and Blakeley Ave/Green Lane top right.

One of the new pilots to be trained on the Tiger Moths of No. 28 Elementary Flying Training School at Pendeford, Wilf Blick, who was to finish his training in South Africa and went on to fly Blenheims in the Western desert.

Local ATC cadets examining a RAF de Havilland Dominie at nearby RAF Cosford.

Twelve Boulton Paul riggers and fitters, and AID inspectors who worked a total of 1025.75 hours in one week to get the first Fairey Barracuda ready for flight on 12 September 1942. Back row, left to right: S. Tillett, J. Houdcroft, A. Bersin, A. Hickmott, T. Broomhall, G. Kilhams. Front row: A. Jones, R. Farmer, J. Tillotson, P. Blunkell, F. Topping, J. Taylor.

An aerial view of the Boulton Paul factory in the centre, with the new RAF airport buildings at the top, and the airfield on the right. Note the anti-aircraft gun site on Pendeford Hill and Pendeford Hall to the left.

Pendeford Lane before it was widened and straightened. The cottage in the background was demolished when this was done. The truck is a Boulton Paul vehicle which has come to investigate an accident.

The front of the Boulton Paul factory just after the war. The massed ranks of bike sheds have all been demolished to make way for more car parking space.

Young apprentices in the Boulton Paul drawing office in 1950. Left to right: Reg Turner, Charlie -?-, Cyril Plimmer, John Green, Brian Holmes, Norman Williams.

A prototype Merlin-engined Balliol being prepared in 1948. Left to right: Dickie Day, Jack Holmes, Owen Brown, George Franks. Note the Wellington bomber behind, one of 270 which were overhauled and converted to navigation trainers.

The Balliol prototype, VS899, in 1948 having its Merlin engine ground run by the Rolls Royce representative at Boulton Paul, Joe Plant. The flight shed alongside has now gone but the wood shop behind is still in use.

The Boulton Paul P.111 experimental delta-wing jet on the taxiway to the airfield at Pendeford in 1951. Note the Wellington T.10 navigation trainer outside the flight shed in the background, and the camouflage which has still not worn off the factory.

George Clayton, a foreman at Boulton Paul, with his Standard Vanguard car. Boulton Paul made the spot-welding rigs for the Vanguard and pressed the body panels. They still press body panels for a wide variety of vehicles.

The manager of Wolverhampton Airport, when it was run by Don Everall (Aviation) Ltd, Eric Holden (left) with R.J.H. Parkes and one of the Club's Piper Colts.

Jack Holmes, taking advantage of flying tuition subsidised by Boulton Paul in the back seat of one of Don Everall's Tiger Moths, G-ANJK.

Boulton Paul's Print Room staff in the early sixties. Left to right: Mrs Mackie, Margaret McKay, Mrs Taylor, Mrs O'Connor, Margaret Bladen, Mrs Gregory, Jack Chambers, Mrs Leadham, Kath Wickstead, Mrs Davies, Mrs Robinson.

Boulton Paul staff admire a Hillman Imp the prize in the 'Win an Imp' contest for the best idea of 1964. I have been unable to find out what the idea was and who had it. In the background can be seen Canberra gun-packs.

The Boulton Paul cricket team in the 1960s.

Some of those attending a Royal Aeronautical Society lecture at Boulton Paul in 1962 given by Fred Crocombe (centre) Chief Designer at Boulton Paul. Earlier he was at Blackburn & General Aircraft where he designed the Beverly. Holding a section of spar is Alf Charlton and with him, holding a cigar, is Jack Freeman, both ex-Norwich men who helped build the R.101 airship, among other things.

A Blackburn Beverly with Bushbury Hill and Pendeford High School in the background. This was the biggest aircraft ever to land at Pendeford Airport and is seen here at an air show in 1965. Its position in the picture corresponds, more or less, to the present position of Safeway's car park!

Don Everall's Auster Autocrat G-AIBZ, a long term resident at Pendeford. The control tower is in the background. It looks rather forlorn, as well it might, the airport closed in 1970 and this area is now covered with bricks and mortar.

Seven

Whitmore Reans

Forming the inner boundary of the area covered by this book, Whitmore Reans is familiar to the people of Codsall and Claregate as an area they would pass through to travel to the centre of Wolverhampton, to work or to shop. At its inner side is the large, Victorian, West Park, formerly Wolverhampton Racecourse.

In addition the huge Courtaulds factory which was built on the site of Dunstall Hall in the 1920s provided employment for many local residents, and even more who moved to the area seeking work. The three main chimneys of Courtaulds, the Three Sisters, were the dominant physical feature of the area for any years, until they were demolished, followed by the factory itself, to be replaced by another housing estate.

An aerial view of Wolverhampton's West Park, which marks the inner boundary of the area covered by this book, *c.* 1926. The bus to Codsall via Claregate would pass along Newhampton Road, in the top left hand corner of the picture. Albert Road is at the foot of the picture.

The Conservatory in West Park around 1909. The Park remains one of the finest surviving Victorian Parks in the country. The conservatory has recently been restored as part of a large renovation programme.

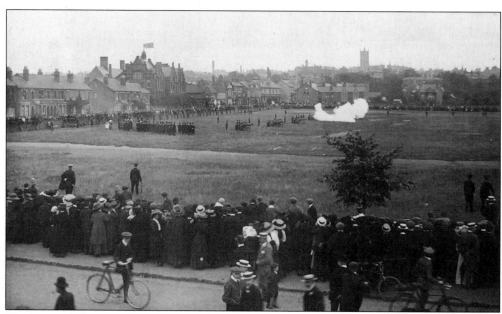

The Territorial Army fire the salute on Coronation Day, 1911. The flag flies on the Municipal Grammar School building on Newhampton Road.

COURTAULD'S (WOLVERHAMPTON) F.C.

Courtaulds Ltd purchased land at Dunstall Park in 1922 on the site of Dunstall Hall and construction of their large factory started in 1924. This is their football team in the 1930s. Back row, left to right: A. Mercer (Sec.), J. Crisp (Chairman), F. Jephson, W. Mansell, I. Ward, S. Spittle, J. Brown, W. Deakin, W. Baker (Trainer). Front row: A. Metcalfe, E. Jacques (Capt.), G. Franks, D. Wright, D. Lapworth.

A Boulton Paul Defiant flying over Courtaulds during the War. The racecourse and the canal can be seen above the aircraft. During the War, Courtaulds built Defiant centre sections under a sub-contract.

Courtaulds Home Guard, 'A' Company of the 20th Staffs. (Wolverhampton) Battalion, in Jackson Street, Whitmore Reans.

Courtaulds nursing staff during the war. Left to right: Nurse Barratt, Sister Warton, Sister Francis, Nurse Phoenix.

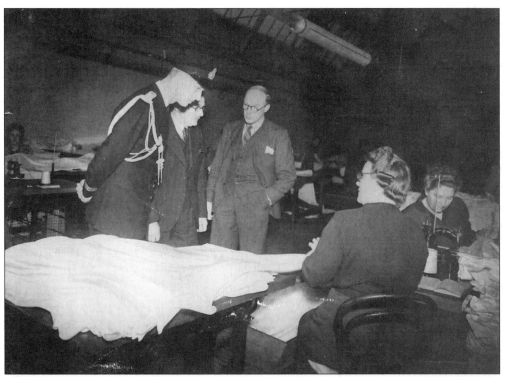

The Duke of Edinburgh visiting Courtaulds during 1948. Alongside him are Mr Dawson and Mr Ratcliffe.

The Duke in the coning section, showing an interest in the places he visits and in characteristic hands behind his back pose.

Frank Tranter, Courtaulds' chauffeur, congratulating Nurse Barratt on passing her driving test in 1950. She had practised on Courtaulds network of private roads.

The float 'Stone-age Aviation' built by Boulton Paul apprentices in 1948 and waiting by West Park. The head of the dragon turned, the mouth opened and apprentices were inside flapping the wings and hurling bags of flour. Gordon Elwell was the driver of the Boulton Paul truck.

5.10 p.m.   **Event 29**
                    FINAL, LONG JUMP, MEN

No.   Name
15   M. Dawson
9   W. Forrest
1   G. Bergmanis
27   N. C. Handley
28   P. Dickenson
29   J. D. Masefield

1.................... 2.................... 3....................

Distance ....

5.15 p.m.   **Event 30**
          FINAL, 80 YARDS SKIPPING RACE, LADIES

1.................... 2.................... 3....................

5.20 p.m.   **Event 31**
     FINAL, 440 YDS. INTER-DEPARTMENTAL RELAY, MEN

1.................... 2....................

Time....................

5.25 p.m.   **Event 32**
    FINAL, 440 YDS. INTER-DEPARTMENTAL RELAY, LADIES

1.................... 2....................

Time....................

5.30 p.m.   **Event 33**
     FINAL, INTER-DEPARTMENTAL TUG-OF-WAR

Winners....................

5.35 p.m.   **Event 34**
     FINAL, 80 YARDS HANDICAP SACK RACE, MEN

No.	Name	Start	No.	Name	Start
17	A. Smith	Scr.	38	F. Walters	17
29	J. D. Masefield	10	21	F. McDonnugh	18
28	P. Dickenson	11	18	D. Butler	20
24	T. Swatman	13	44	M. C. J. Bird	20

1.................... 2.................... 3....................

5.40 p.m.   **Event 35**
     HEATS, 60 YARDS SACK RACE, LADIES
     First and Second in each Heat to run in Final

Heat 1		Heat 2		Heat 3	
No.	Name	No.	Name	No.	Name
101	M. Munday	102	F. Edwards	109	B. Kelleher
111	N. Cox	116	M. Loftus	119	I. Howells
126	B. Myles	120	I. Humphries	128	L. Wolfe
131	A. Iwanown	135	G. Berry	137	P. Matthews
138	P. Fisher	139	J Potts	140	C. Wright
145	V. Ford	141	S. Edens	142	P. Jervis
146	I. Hamil	143	M. McLoughlin	144	J. Stanley
123	D. Pugh				

1.......... 2..........   1.......... 2..........   1.......... 2..........

A page from the Courtaulds Sports and Social Club official programme for the annual sports on 9 July 1949. The programme also included the 'Men's pillow fight' and the 'Gents Knobbly Knees contest', neither of the them exactly Olympic events, yet! However, a basketball match against Leicester was the semi-final of the All England Championship.

The retirement of Sister Marsh and Sister Round at Courtaulds. Sister Warton is between them. Standing, left to right, are: R. Lily Biggs, Nurse Betts, Nurse Douglas, Nurse Healey, Nurse Lloyd, Nurse Reynolds, Nurse Barratt, Nurse Cooper, Bessie Newton.

Courtaulds own shunting engine *Dafydd*, a Peckett 0-4-0 saddle tank, which had been built for the Flint factory, hence the Welsh name. Courtaulds had a huge coal yard next to Hordern Road, fed from the Oxley to Wombourne line, through Aldersley.

A Sunbeam F4 trolley bus in Court Road, Whitmore Reans, waiting to set off on Route 2 to Darlaston via Bilston. One of Courtaulds three chimneys (The Three Sisters) is visible behind, as is a Co-op electric bread van doing a three point turn.

A Sunbeam trolley bus coming along Hordern Road from the Courtaulds entrance in the summer of 1963. This is the No. 7 which ran the opposite way round Whitmore Reans to the No. 2. The trolley buses ceased on this route in August 1965.

The retirement of Harold Jones, chargehand foreman in Courtaulds, in the early 1960s. Left to right: B. Sanders, Bill Davies, T. Wittingham, -?-, S. Richardson, A. Bayliss, Eric Willis, Harold Jones, H. Fullard, H. Darby, Syd Bayliss, A. Stead, C. Small, Tony Stafford, Dave Hunt, Dave -?-, D. Simpson, N. Collins, A. Picken, W. French, F. Davies.

Crowds gathered to see one of the Courtaulds Three Sisters coming down on 17 June 1973. The explosions have just been fired. This was one of two 365 ft stacks. The third was 260 ft.

A few seconds later and 5,000 tons of bricks are just about to hit the ground. This picture was taken from the racecourse. The building on the left is a water tower.

The Second Year Juniors at St Andrews Primary School, Whitmore Reans, in the year 1978/79. Their class teacher, Wendy Landman, is at the rear on the left, and the headteacher, Mr Goodwin, is on the right.

The Nativity Play at Whitmore Reans Primary School at Christmas 1976.

Eight

Oxley Moor
and Dunstall Park

The 'green lung' of Wolverhampton is a large area of sporting facilities which are not usually associated with one another as they are split into three by railway and canal. There is the former Autherley Farm, now the Aldersley Stadium complex, but on the south side of the canal, there are also Oxley Moor, with Oxley Park Golf Course and the nature reserve of the former Oxley Sidings, and Dunstall Park, since 1886 Wolverhampton's racecourse.

Development has skirted this area, along the Stafford road, and nibbling at Dunstall Park on the Whitmore Reans side, but it is still possible to walk along the tow-path from the Stafford road to the site of the lost village of Aldersley, and find oneself at a quiet backwater of trees and fields, yet with Wolverhampton's suburbs on all sides.

Oxley Manor, which was situated in the area between what is now Oxley Park Gold Course and the Stafford road. It was owned for a while by Sir Alexander Stavely Hill after he sold Dunstall Park to be redeveloped as a racecourse.

Two elephants grazing on Oxley Moor! Around 1928-9 there were no houses on the west side of Stafford road, residents on the other side could see the Wrekin with no houses in sight. These elephants were probably from a circus at Dunstall Park and the man on the bike has paused while riding on the Stafford road between Manor Road and Burnham Avenue.

The tram terminus on the Oxley Bank on the Stafford road which was just at the start of Bushbury Lane. The entrance to Oxley House is on the left.

Almost the same view before the tram tracks had been laid. The baby in the pram was Ron Hudson.

An aerial view of Oxley taken in 1941 with the Three Tuns junction near the top right. Elston Hall School is at the top left. The roads running to the right from Winchester Road are Harrowby Road and Sandon Road, named after Boulton Paul directors.

The stables at Dunstall Park Racecourse between the wars. The racecourse had opened in 1886 replacing the earlier one on the site of West Park.

The parade ring at Dunstall Park with one of only nine Churchwood 2-8-0 express freight locomotives (No. 47XX) going over the Dunstall viaduct towards Oxley Sidings.

INSPECTING THE FLYING MACHINES AT DUNSTALL PARK.

In June 1910 Dunstall Park hosted the first All British flying meeting and these hangars were built alongside the canal beyond which can be seen Oxley Sidings. The first two house the aircraft of Claude Graham White and Cecil Grace.

COL. CODY.

Dunstall Park. Wolverhampton.

One of a series of postcards produced to commemorate the meeting. Unfortunately, S.F. Cody, though entered, did not make it because of a crash just before the meeting. The photographer superimposed a drawing of his aircraft on a contemporary picture of the racecourse.

A race at Dunstall Park around 1930 showing the Courtaulds chimneys alongside the track. As can be seen, rather than Three Sisters, there were actually four.

A BR Standard Class 4, 2-6-0 locomotive No.76088, getting underway in the Oxley coaling stage. This engine was transferred from Oxley in 1967.

An ex-GWR 0-6-0 pannier tank shunting engine in Oxley Sidings before 1966. The sidings used to be very extensive, with two levels, as can be seen in this photograph. They have now been greatly reduced in size and the disused part has become a wild-life preserve.

Old steam locomotives come to die in the Oxley Sidings, northern end, in the mid sixties. A Brittania Stanier No.70445, is in the foreground with a BR Standard Stanier, a Black 5, Class 5, and a 264 Tank engine.

The author in 1953, age 5 years 9 months, outside the family cottage in Oaken about to hunt for rustlers and desperadoes in the surrounding fields and lanes.

Acknowledgements

Happily I did not need a shotgun and a pair of six-shooters when I set out to collect photographs for this book! I am very grateful for the kindness and helpfulness of the people who loaned me photographs. I was brought up in Oaken and Codsall and now live in Claregate and it was delightful talking to people about the way things were and especially in talking to people who knew my father, grandfather and great-grandfather.

Many of the photographs came from two important collections. Firstly, I must thank the Codsall and Bilbrook Civic Society for access to their superb collection and especially to David Holden for spending long hours going through them with me and allowing me to benefit from his extensive knowledge of them. In addition I borrowed many photographs from the Dowty Boulton Paul Archives, administered by the Boulton Paul Association. The area covered by this book contains thousands of people who worked at Boulton Paul or who had relatives there.

The two photographs of Aldersley Junction are from the Arthur Watts Collection in the British Waterways Archive.

Individuals who loaned me photographs either directly, or indirectly through the Codsall Civic Society, and the Boulton Paul Association, were:

Miss Barratt, David Bate, John Bishop, Harry Blewitt, Wilf Blick, John and Leah Brew, Peter Brew, Brenda Broome, Mrs D. Brown, Miss M. Burd, Miss P. Burd, Claregate Garage, Arthur Colley, Sheila Collins, Ron Cooper, Peter Dewey, Simon Dewey, the Gaskell family, Mrs V. Farnath, Samantha Hall, Nigel Heath, Mrs M.J. Heath, Brain Holmes, Jack Holmes, B. Hodson, Mrs D. Housden, Graham Hughes, Hannah Landman, Harry Law, David Lee of Claregate School, Chris Martin, Wendy Matthiason, Robert Mee, Donald Morris, Doug Nicholson, Palmer's Cross School, John Pendrous, A. Picken, Cyril Plimmer, Mrs Reynaert, Doreen Seiboth, Andy Simpson, Tony Stafford, Vera Taylor, the Twentyman family, Mrs B. Walker, Mrs Wilkinson.

I sincerely hope I have not missed anyone out but if I have, I apologise.